D0891804

Responsible Pet Care

Gerbils

Responsible Pet Care

Gerbils

TINA HEARNE

Rourke Publications, Inc.
Vero Beach, FL 32964

Typical posture of
Mongolian gerbil, with
tail being used for
balance.

Library of Congress Cataloging-in-Publication Data

Hearne, Tina.
  Gerbils/by Tina Hearne.

      p. cm - (Responsible pet care)
  Includes index.
  Summary: Examines the different varieties of gerbils and describes how they may be housed, exercised, handled, fed, cleaned, and bred.
  ISBN 0-86625-186-3
  1. Gerbils as pets - Juvenile literature. [1. Gerbils.] I. Title.
II. Series.
SF459.G4H38 1989
636'.932'33-dc19   88-37902
                                      CIP
                                      AC

CONTENTS

Why Choose A Gerbil?

The Mongolian gerbil is one of the most popular of the pet rodents: attractive, alert, and acrobatic. This active pet becomes quite tame when handled regularly from an early age. It is a **social animal** and always interesting to watch. The gerbil explores all the opportunities for climbing and burrowing that the responsible owner provides.

The Mongolian gerbil is attractive, alert, and acrobatic. Note the black claws, which are a characteristic of the species. The sandy colored coat, fading to white on the underside, is typical.

As a desert animal, the Mongolian gerbil urinates very little, and its accommodation stays dry and odorless. This variety is the Gray Agouti.

Gerbils make good indoor pets and are very suitable to keep in an apartment. Give them a stimulating environment, using either a good cage or a tank. As desert animals, gerbils living in the wild have to be economical with water in order to survive. This trait is an advantage when they live in captivity. They urinate very little, and their accommodation stays dry and odorless.

The accommodation must be very secure. If they were allowed to escape, gerbils could establish wild colonies in some parts of America where conditions were favorable. They might become a threat to agriculture. For this reason, they are prohibited as pets in some states. Check that your Department of Agriculture has no such ban.

One of the few drawbacks of keeping this agreeable animal is that it has a short life span. No gerbil is likely to live much more than three years. You will have to come to terms with this unhappy fact. In return for the pleasure gerbils give you, make sure you provide them with a high quality of life during the few years they are with you.

Varieties

The gerbil lives wild in the deserts of **Mongolia**. This animal has only been kept as a pet for the last twenty-five years. In contrast, the rabbit has been domesticated for hundreds of years and the cat and dog for thousands of years. One effect of this short period of captivity is that only a few varieties exist. Breeders have not yet had time to develop many different kinds.

As a result, most gerbils have the normal coloration of the wild species, *Meriones unguiculatus*. The coat is sand colored, with a distinct yellow tinge. It is made up of two separate types of fur. Close to the body is the short underhair, which is gray in color. On the back this hair is dark gray; on the underside it shades to pale gray or white. The golden color of the coat comes from the long guard hairs, which are a mixture of black and gold. Black claws, a black line along the length of the tail, and a black tuft at its tip are distinguishing features of the Mongolian gerbil.

Most Mongolian gerbils retain the natural coloration of the wild species.

8

The first mutation to appear in captivity was the albino. When the black appeared, it was possible to breed gerbils that are gray in color.

The first mutation to appear in captivity was the albino, which is pure white. Another early variety was the cinnamon, which is the same as the normal variety but without the long guard hairs. The cinnamon is paler in color than the normal variety. A newer variety to appear in America is the black gerbil. It has been useful in breeding a range of gray gerbils.

The Gerbilarium

In the Mongolian desert, gerbils live underground and are accustomed to the security of burrows. The most natural way to keep them in captivity is to allow them to live in a similar way, although of course on a smaller scale.

The best accommodation is a large tank containing a mixture of peat and chopped straw. This is called a gerbilarium. The burrowing medium should be compacted as much as possible by pressing it down to make a solid hill. The gerbils will spend hours excavating their own tunnels. They will also make an underground nest where they will sleep and rear their young. If clean paper toweling is put in the tank, the adult gerbils will drag it into the burrows and shred it into comfortable bedding.

In the wild, gerbils live underground in desert country. Their burrows provide security, shelter, and good insulation against the heat of the desert day, and the cold of its night.

When kept in captivity, gerbils are best kept in a gerbilarium, like this one. Here they have the opportunity to excavate burrows in a tank half filled with a peat and straw mixture. Like all animals that naturally live underground, they need the privacy that a cage cannot provide.

Fill the tank only halfway with the burrowing medium. In this way the gerbils can be above ground or underground, as they choose. Provide some branches to give them opportunities for climbing. This will keep the gerbils happily occupied.

Use a well ventilated cover on the tank. Wire mesh covers are sold for this purpose, but a perforated one would also be suitable.

Keep the gerbilarium out of direct sunlight to prevent overheating. The extensive burrows the gerbils dig in the wild protect them from the heat of the desert day and the cold of its night. Remember, the small burrows they dig in the confines of a tank do not insulate them from the surrounding temperature to the same extent. You must be sure the room they are kept in does not get too hot or too cold.

Cages

You may also keep gerbils in a cage, positioned out of drafts and direct sunlight. Since the gerbils will spend most of their lives in it, always select the biggest cage available. It gives the gerbils as much living space as possible and allows you to create an interesting environment for your pets.

Commercial cages will be made of metal or plastic. Homemade cages are usually constructed of timber, but they must be sturdy enough to withstand the gnawing of these **rodent animals**. Covering exposed timber ledges with metal can protect them from destruction.

A system of ramps, shelves, and galleries will act as a substitute for the burrows of the natural environment and provide a route for the gerbils to use when moving around the cage. In this way the gerbils use the maximum amount of space, rather than just the floor area.

Two gerbils are being installed in a new cage. Most commercial cages like this one are easy to clean, but they are very small for such active animals. A strongly built homemade cage may be far superior.

This Ivory Mongolian gerbil examines its multi-story commercial cage. This kind of cage can provide suitable accommodation, but the starter pack alone is insufficient.

Burrowing animals must be given sleeping quarters where they can feel as safe and secure as they would underground. A nest box with some soft bedding, such as hay, is therefore an essential piece of cage furniture.

Most cages are designed to contain a layer of burrowing material in the base. This is important, because it allows the gerbils to bolt out of sight when they feel the need and to indulge their natural instinct to burrow. Cardboard and white paper, for instance, can be provided for shredding. All but the youngest gerbils will be able to tear up such materials and gradually add to the layer.

13

Exercise

Gerbils are very active creatures. It would be cruel not to give them plenty of opportunity for exercise. In the wild they run, jump, climb, and burrow. A good gerbilarium or cage should contain facilities for them to exercise in these ways, even on a much reduced scale. Every gerbil owner must provide such living accommodation for their pets.

This gerbil is being taken out of its cage to give it a change of scene and a wider area to explore.

Gerbils will use lengths of piping in the cage or exercise pen as substitute burrows. They will be able to dart out of sight when disturbed.

An exercise wheel can be useful, and those of the solid type may be recommended. Often gerbils will run many miles each day on a wheel. It is sometimes reported that an animal has been caught on a wheel by the tail or by a foot. Such accidents are quite rare. Most owners feel that the advantages of an exercise wheel outweigh the slight risk. You must decide for yourself.

Owners often take their gerbils out of their cages or tanks for short periods each day. This is a good idea, since it gives the gerbils a change of scene and more opportunity to move around.

Sometimes it is possible to provide an exercise pen for outside. An outdoor pen should be built with a solid floor, because some gerbils develop sore **hocks** if kept on a wire floor. The mesh on the sides must, of course, be small enough to prevent escape. Lengths of piping in the pen can act as substitute burrows. The gerbils will use them as bolt holes if they are disturbed and feel vulnerable.

Handling

Small rodents such as the gerbil are easily tamed if they are handled frequently when young. If more than one person is going to handle the gerbil, agree which method of handling you will all use. Be consistent, so that the gerbil understands what to do. Be gentle, so that the gerbil is not alarmed or distressed by rough or too frequent handling.

Some owners hold out a hand and just let the gerbil walk on to it. Since these creatures are naturally inquisitive, this usually works. Once the gerbil is on your hand, gently close the other hand over the gerbil's back. Gerbils can also be cupped in the hands, like any other small creature.

Pet gerbils are inquisitive creatures. Because this boy is sitting down, his pet is not likely to come to any harm. The gerbil is a good climber and can cling to the boy's clothing with its long claws.

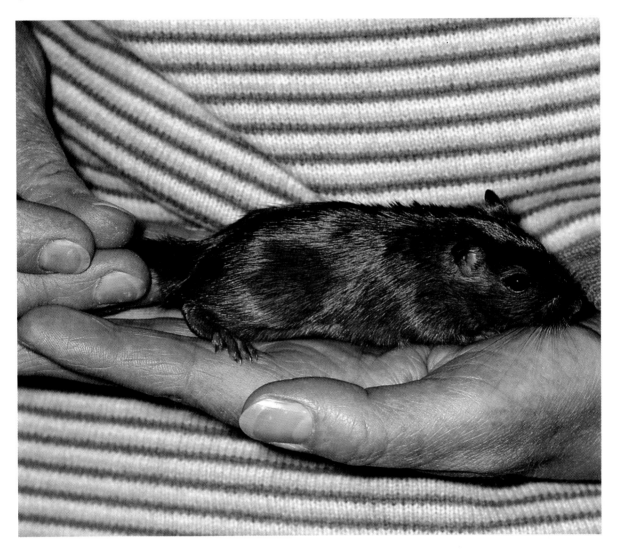

Let your gerbil become used to being handled from an early age. Take care not to let it fall, and handle the tail very gently.

Always hold a gerbil facing you. Gerbils may be frightened by a sudden movement elsewhere in the room that you hardly notice. Once alarmed, a gerbil may leap from your hand and hurt itself falling. By holding it facing you, it will fall on you and can cling to your clothing.

Never pick up a gerbil by the tail. In fact, avoid handling the tail at all, particularly the tip. An undamaged tail will have a black tuft of fur at the tip. This fur can be stripped off accidentally by careless handling. In the wild it is a safety device. A fleeing gerbil, caught by its predator at the tip of the tail, can shed the tip and escape with its life.

Feeding

Many of the food mixtures available commercially are excellent. These are made up of grains such as wheat, corn, oats, and barley, and also canary and sunflower seeds. Such a mixture contains protein, fats, and carbohydrate, together with certain vitamins and minerals. It forms the basis of a satisfactory diet for gerbils.

Always supplement a commercial food with plenty of fruits and vegetables, offered fresh each day. Individual gerbils will develop particular likes and dislikes, but provide as wide a range of foods as possible for good nutrition and for interest. Hay is also a good food, and most gerbils love it.

Gerbils may take an occasional slice of hard boiled egg or even a spoonful of cat or dog food. Although mainly **herbivorous**, they are able to digest animal products.

Fresh drinking water must be provided daily. As desert animals, gerbils use water economically, but the amount they use each day is vital to their health.

Sunflower seeds are a great favorite with gerbils, but a good diet consists of a variety of grains and seeds.

Gerbils should be fed every day, because they will not **hoard** food in captivity as will hamsters. About one tablespoonful of the basic mixture a day is usually the right amount for each adult. They should also have fresh water daily. Although they will receive some water in the fresh fruits and vegetables you put out, you must still refill the water bottle each day.

Even though gerbils are desert animals, they cannot go without water. Gerbilariums and cages can easily overheat, causing the gerbils to suffer dehydration. They are far better protected in the desert, where their burrows are deep enough to remain at a constant temperature and humidity. In captivity they must rely on their owners for protection from heat and dryness.

19

Grooming And Cleaning

Gerbils kept in clean, dry accommodations need very little help in grooming. If two are kept together, they will groom each other. This happens whether they are a breeding pair or a pair of females. This attractive trait is called social grooming.

Occasionally overgrown claws may need attention, but constant digging and scratching normally keeps them in trim. Your most important contribution is to check for signs of soreness around the mouth, eyes, or hocks. These are vulnerable areas for all burrowing rodents. Also check for signs of fighting such as scratches or wounds, and for **parasites**.

Cleaning the cage or gerbilarium is, of course, one of your main responsibilities. Check the gerbilarium each day. Remove uneaten fruit and vegetable matter. Refill the water bottle, and check to be sure it is not leaking. Gerbils urinate so little that the highly absorbent burrowing material will remain clean and odorless for two or three months at a time. When it does need changing, move the gerbils to safe, temporary accommodations. Completely empty out the peat and straw mixture, and after washing and drying the tank, replace it with a fresh supply.

Gerbils are fastidious about their personal hygiene, keeping themselves clean and odorless.

When two gerbils are kept together, they will often groom each other. This attractive trait is known as social grooming.

Cages need to be cleaned more often. Attend to them every day, and clean them thoroughly once a week. Although hygiene is very important do not disturb your animals more than necessary. There is usually no reason to change the bedding, and it is wise to return some of the shredded litter after cleaning. This reduces the stress that gerbils may feel when their home is seriously disturbed.

Breeding

If you plan to keep a breeding pair, select healthy, unrelated gerbils and house them together from the age of about seven weeks. Attempts to introduce gerbils to each other after the age of ten weeks frequently fail. An introduction as late as this can lead to serious fighting.

Do not keep a breeding pair of gerbils unless you are confident that you will be able to find good homes for the young. Under ideal conditions gerbils are likely to be prolific breeders. In theory, a pair can produce a litter every month. The average pair produces six or seven litters in their lifetime. Some produce only three or four while others have as many as ten litters. Each litter will contain an average of four to six babies.

These babies are only half an hour old. By thirty days old their eyes will open and they will have fur.

When a litter is born, leave the whole family together.

Pregnancy lasts about twenty-four days. During this time you may notice that the female drinks more water than usual and puts on weight. Feed her top quality food with a high protein content. For extra nourishment, add some dried skimmed milk powder to her diet.

Both male and female gerbils are good parents. There is no need to remove the male after the birth of the litter. Parents and babies will live together as a family. The parents should be supplied with clean paper to shred for bedding material. The gerbils need privacy at this time. Do not interfere with the nest at all. Any disturbance can be very stressful and may even cause the mother to turn against her young.

The Young

Baby gerbils are often born at night, and a faint crying sound is the only clue you may have. Do not disturb them. Any attempt to uncover the nest to look at the babies can result in their being eaten by the mother.

As you would expect, babies born after such a short pregnancy are small, undeveloped, and helpless. At first they have dark red skins. They have no hair until it begins to grow in the second week of life. The eyes open in the third week.

Gradually the young gerbils become stronger and bolder and start to explore their environment. They may safely be left to the care of their own parents, who will bundle them back into the nest if they become too adventurous.

There are six baby gerbils in this litter. The babies are born after a pregnancy of only twenty-four days, and are consequently very helpless at first. Their eyes open during the third week of life.

The young are weaned at the age of three or four weeks. They can live together in a colony until six or eight weeks from birth, but then must be housed separately to avoid fighting and interbreeding.

Newborn gerbils stay close to their mother and are nursed by her for at least three weeks, often four. Only if she is expecting another litter right away will a mother gerbil remove her young from the nest as early as three weeks after birth.

As they develop, young gerbils begin to try solid food. One good food to feed them at this time is the special rearing mixture sold for young canaries. Small seeds are also suitable.

Normally young gerbils are safe living together to the age of six to eight weeks. After this their playful fighting turns serious and they must be put in new homes. They become adults at between nine and twelve weeks of age.

25

Ailments

Wounds sustained in fighting can be severe: gerbils fight to the death. If this happens, seek veterinary help for deep wounds, and bathe surface lesions with an antiseptic. Most important, separate the fighting animals by placing them in different cages.

Many gerbils like to gnaw, and gnawing can cause soreness of the mouth and nose. Gnawing cage bars, for instance, can be very damaging. Try providing a natural material such as a log of wood instead, or large nuts with their shells intact. If you cannot break the gerbil's habit you will have to put it in a different home, for instance, one without bars to gnaw.

Burrowing can also cause soreness of the mouth and nose, and some gerbils get eye infections from burrowing. Burrowing in a dusty medium may give rise to an allergic reaction including sneezing and runny eyes. Substitute a better burrowing medium and seek veterinary advice if the condition persists.

Gerbils will fight to the death. It is difficult to pair up adults even for breeding, so never expect to be able to house gerbils together unless they have been paired by the age of about seven weeks.

This black gerbil is in fine condition. Gerbils are generally very healthy when kept clean, dry, and warm, but have poor powers of recuperation once they fall ill.

Heat exhaustion can be caused by positioning the tank or cage in direct sunlight. Reduce the temperature at once by moving the tank or cage or screening it from the sun. Increase the ventilation, and provide water to counteract dehydration. Leave the gerbil undisturbed to recover in its own time.

Some gerbils suffer from fits brought on by stress. These fits can be fatal, and the only treatment is to give the gerbil its privacy. The condition is thought to be hereditary, so be sure not to breed any gerbils that have had fits.

There is no specific gerbil flea, but gerbils sometimes catch cat or dog fleas. Treat the cat or dog, and in particular their bedding, where the fleas breed, rather than the gerbil.

Health and Longevity

Gerbils are generally healthy. The most obvious sign of good health is the speed and agility of their movement. Normally, busy periods of digging, burrowing, and playing are alternated with quiet rest periods.

Another sign of good health is a high level of inquisitiveness. At its best, a gerbil will always eagerly explore new items in its environment, whether in or out of its tank or cage. A gerbil will often find creative and intelligent ways of using new items. This is the trait that makes gerbils such fascinating creatures to observe.

A high level of activity, such as digging, burrowing, playing, and collecting nesting material, as this gerbil is doing, is healthy.

Another sign of good health is a high level of curiosity. It is natural for a gerbil to take a keen interest in any new item in its environment. This appealing inquisitiveness should last the whole of the gerbil's short life.

In health, the gerbil will remain clean and free from parasites. Its coat will be glossy with no areas of baldness. There should be no soreness, particularly around the mouth, hocks, or ears. The eyes of a healthy animal will be bright, clean, and undamaged, with no sign of inflammation. The appetite will be good; the droppings small and dry. It is normal for urine to be used to mark the gerbil's own territory.

Like other small rodents, such as hamsters and mice, gerbils have short lives. They also have poor powers of recovery once they fall ill. At such a time, prompt veterinary attention is essential if there is to be any hope of preventing a rapid deterioration.

A gerbil's health is very dependent on its living conditions. Those kept in clean, dry accommodations and fed a high quality diet are likely to attain their full life span of about three years.

GLOSSARY

Herbivorous	Feeding on plants only.
Hoard	To store up for later use.
Hock	The lower joint in the back of a gerbil's leg.
Mongolia	A country in Asia that borders on China and the Soviet Union.
Mutation	A genetic change that is passed on to the next generation.
Parasites	Fleas and other organisms that live on the blood of other animals.
Rodent animals	Members of the Rodentia order, small mammals that gnaw (Latin *rodere*, to gnaw). Rodents have front (incisor) teeth that grow continuously. This order includes mice, squirrels, beavers, gerbils, and many other familiar animals.
Social animals	Animals that prefer being with companions to being alone.

INDEX

We would like to thank and acknowledge the following people for the use of their photographs and transparencies:

Cover	Jane Burton/Bruce Coleman Ltd
Title Page	M Gilroy/Aquila Photographics Ltd
P. 6/7	Jane Burton/Bruce Coleman Ltd
	M Gilroy/Aquila Photographics Ltd
P. 8/9	Hans Reinhard/Bruce Coleman Ltd
	Aquila Photographics Ltd
P. 10/11	Carol Hughes/Bruce Coleman Ltd
P. 12/13	Sally Anne Thompson/Animal Photography
	M. Gilroy/Aquila Photographics Ltd
P. 14/15	Sally Anne Thompson/RSPCA
	M Gilroy/Aquila Photographics Ltd
P. 16/17	Sally Anne Thompson/Animal Photography
	M Gilroy/Aquila Photographics Ltd
P. 18/19	M Gilroy/Aquila Photographics Ltd
P. 20/21	M Gilroy/Aquila Photographics Ltd
	Aquila Photographics Ltd
P. 22/23	Sally Ann Thompson/RSPCA
P. 24/25	Aquila Photographics Ltd
	Sally Anne Thompson/Animal Photography
P. 26/27	Aquila Photographics Ltd
	Sally Anne Thompson/Animal Photography
P. 28/29	A J Deane/Bruce Coleman Ltd
	M Gilroy/Aquila Photographics Ltd